Greece

*You have kept photos and all sorts of mementoes
from your trips to Paris, and now you find yourself
with a unique collection, enough to awaken
your vocation to become a curator.
So as to avoid your favourite 'exhibits' getting hidden away in
an old shoe box, Elsa Editions is publishing this album
specially to give your souvenirs an ideal setting.*

*This interactive guide takes you back,
in text and pictures, to the atmosphere that gave
each itinerary its special charm.
You can then personalize it by including your own mementoes –
travel cards, museum tickets, restaurant menus, postcards,
bank notes etc. – in the pages designed for them.
You can include your own photos, so that the book becomes
a gentle wave of nostalgia, uniquely your own.*

© 1998 Kingfisher Publications Plc
ISBN : 2-7452-0455-6

Memories

of

Greece

Greece, cradle of Western civilisation

Greece was the stage
upon which legendary struggles
were fought between
mere mortals and the gods
of Olympus. Zeus, the god
of gods, was among
their number as were his brother
Poseidon, god of the seas,
and Hades, the god
of the underworld. Aphrodite,
goddess of beauty and love,
rivalled even Zeus' own consort
Hera. War had its god, Ares,
and wine and the rapture
of intoxication had theirs in the person of Dionysos; no roll
could omit the sun-god Apollo, nor his twin sister Artemis.

But, above all, this country
is the birthplace of some of the
greatest creations of the human
spirit. Greece's contribution
to the spheres of art, philosophy
and politics have made it
the cradle of Western civilisation.

Athens, history of an ancient city

*The monuments
of the Acropolis
towering high
above the city
of Athens are the
fruit of the determination of
one man: Pericles, the famous
Fifth century BC, statesman
who, for almost thirty years,
occupied the position
of strategist or First Magistrate of Athens. In 458 BC,
it was he who entrusted the famous sculptor Phidias
with the task of constructing the buildings of the Acropolis
with the help of the finest architects of the day. Greek
theatre also owes a great deal to Pericles, who gave
his support to the great authors of the age — Aeschylus,
Sophocles, Euripides and
Aristophanes. As patron
of the arts, it was thanks
to Pericles that the rest
of the country took up
the Athenian model
which was then known
as "the Greek school".*

The eternal fortress of the Acropolis

*Beyond the Propylaea rises
the Parthenon, the very symbol
of Athens' greatness
in the Fifth century BC.*

*The Athena Parthenos was consecrated in 438 BC.
This gold and ivory statue sculpted by Phidias,
which measured some fifteen metres in height, depicted
the goddess standing upright, holding a Victory
some two metres high in her right hand and a spear
in her left hand. This statue stood
inside the Parthenon, the temple
dedicated to the city's guardian
goddess Athena.*

The portico of the **Caryatids**, masterpiece of Hellenic art

Facing the Parthenon, there
stands the Erechtheion, one
of the most important places
of worship on the Acropolis.
Now completely restored, this
temple was the shrine
of the city's legendary founder
Cecrops. His tomb is surmounted
by a sort of funerary dais which is a masterpiece
of Hellenic art – the portico of the Caryatids.

Athena, goddess of wisdom, and Poseidon, god
of the seas, were also worshipped in the Erechtheion.
Regarded as the most precious gift ever made

to humankind by the gods, the olive
tree given by Athena was preserved
in this temple. The building
which exists today is said
to occupy the sacred site
where the goddess fought
against Poseidon.

The island of Aegina,
wonder of the Saronic Gulf

The island of Aegina is thought
to have been the birthplace
of the great comic dramatist
Aristophanes. Famous for its
pistachios, Aegina also produces
a celebrated retsina wine.
Aegina has beautiful sand
beaches to offer its many visitors,
but above all it has one
of the most important temples
in the Ancient World which
is also one of the best preserved
in all Greece: the temple
of Aphaia. This mysterious Doric
order shrine is thought to date from the Fifth century BC.
In 1901 archaeologists found a Sixth century inscription
there dedicated to an ancient deity
of Aegina, Aphaia, goddess
of wisdom and light, similar
to Athena. The ruins
of the propylaeum, the main
altar, the baths and the priests'
quarters still bear witness
to the importance of this temple.

Cape Sounion, legend and myth …

▶◀▶◀▶◀▶◀▶◀▶◀▶◀▶◀▶◀▶◀▶◀▶

According to legend, it was from the summit of the cape Sounion headland that Aegeus, King of Athens, watched and waited for the return of his son Theseus who had set out to face the Minotaur, a half-man, half-bull monster on the island of Crete. The young man had agreed with his father that he would hoist a white sail to signal that he was returning victorious. But on his return he forgot to give the signal, and a black sail was hoisted in error. Catching sight of the black sail Aegeus thought that his son had lost his life in the encounter. In despair, the king hurled himself from the rocky heights into the sea which bears his name today. The account of Theseus' exploits written by Homer forms part of the founding myths of the history of Crete under the reign of the legendary King Minos.

The Cyclades, pearls of the Aegean sea

The Greek islands, each with its own unique personality, are every bit as inseparable a part of the image of Greece as its capital city, its ancient ruins or its legends. Some much-visited and some unknown to the tourists, scorched by the sun or battered by the winds, these islands compose a symphony of colour, light and beauty which is without

equal anywhere in the world. The archipelago of the Cyclades is made up of a string of islands which offer a wonderfully varied palette of dream landscapes and secret treasures tucked away between their rocky summits and the blue waters of the Aegean sea. From terraced villages to endless beaches and from Venetian mansions to windmills, everything here in the dazzling sunlight delights the eye.

The sacred island of Delos

Legend would have it that the
Cyclades were brought into being
by Poseidon, the Greek god of the sea,
who caused them to rise out
of the waters one fine day with
a mere blow of his trident. Delos,
for its part, began its existence
as a floating rock called Asteria, after
the name of a young girl who flung herself into the sea
in order to flee Zeus' advances. Asteria's sister Leto,
pregnant by Zeus, sought shelter there to give birth
to her child Apollo. The island became a shrine
to the young god of light who was later to build his temple
there (Artemis, Apollo's sister, was born nine days later on
the neighbouring island of Rhenea). Delos was rewarded
by being anchored in the heart of the Cyclades by four

pillars
of diamond
which rose up
out of
the waves ...

Mykonos, island of seduction ...

Mykonos is far and away
the most touristic island
of the archipelago.
It symbolises all
the powers of seduction
which the Greek islands exert upon travellers
the world over. All along its enchanting
shores lie strings of houses of a dazzling white,
while the countryside of the island is scattered here
and there with chapels and windmills.
The little alleyways of Mykonos form a labyrinth where
visitors can enjoy trying to lose themselves while
they dream about the legends which make up at once
both the myth
and history
of the Cyclades.

Santorin, or the myth of Atlantis ...

The story
of Atlantis
was first told by the Athenian
poet Solon and later taken up
once more by the philosopher Plato in one of his famous
dialogues, **Critias, or Of Atlantis.**
According to legend, this fabulous island was swallowed
up as the result of a cataclysm nine hundred years
before Solon's journey which is thought to have taken
place during the Sixth century BC. This date would seem
to coincide with a volcanic eruption
which occurred on the island
of Santorin round about the year
1500 BC, hence the temptation to see
Santorin as the inheritor of this
mythical civilisation. The ruins first
discovered in 1967 and subsequently
uncovered on the site of Akrotirion
have also lent strength to this
hypothesis — at least in the eyes
of those in love with myth …

Delphi, the "navel of the world"

The world-famous tholos of Delphi
stands at Marmaria, whose name
means the "place where marble
is found" in Greek.
A place of mystery and beauty lying
at the foot of Mount Parnassus,
the site of Delphi was the "navel of the world" for over
a thousand years. In the days when the Greeks would
travel there to pay homage to the god Apollo and hear
his oracles … Famous since ancient times for the purity
of its waters and the sweetness of its melody, the spring
of Castalia brought water for the ablutions of the high
priestesses of Apollo while the spring of Cassotis,
for its part, was endowed with powers of divination.

A stroll through the heart of Epirus

To the north-west of Delphi, Epirus is a mountainous
region bathed to the west by the Ionian sea across
which it faces the island of Corfu. It has retained many
traces of its ancient inhabitants and former occupants;
the old city of Ioánnina, for example, bears
the marks of its domination
by the Ottomans from the Fifteenth
to the Nineteenth centuries.

In the heart
of the region of Zagoria
in Epirus lies the Vikos Gorge, where
the river Vikos offers a striking
spectacle as it runs tightly hemmed
in between two limestone cliffs
several hundred metres high.
The Vikos national park is also home
to bears, chamois, boars and even
lynxes.

Corfu, the greenest of the Greek islands

The most famous of the Ionian
islands is undoubtedly Corfu,
which is distinguished from the rest by the combined
influences of its successive masters. The Venetians,
for example, who occupied the island from the Fourteenth
to the Seventeenth centuries left their lasting mark
upon its architecture.

The island of Corfu was immortalised by Homer
in the **Odyssey** under the name of Phaiakes. It was
in fact off the shores of this island that the hero Ulysses

was shipwrecked while
returning from the Trojan War.
Washed up on the coast he was
taken in by Nausicaä
the daughter of King Alcinous.
Without revealing his true
identity he remained and lived
for a time among the people
of Phaiakes, who became
famous thereafter for their
hospitality, before leaving
to rejoin his own people.

The Meteora monasteries, between heaven and earth …

Perched like eagles' eyries atop
their crags and surrounded
by a breathtaking setting of rocky
peaks, the Meteora monasteries defy
the gulf that yawns
beneath them.
The first of these monasteries were founded
in the Fourteenth century and show clearly
how their members were driven by a thirst
for the absolute. Standing on the most
massive of these rocks is the monastery
of Great Meteoron, which was established
in 1344 by Saint Athanasius and is still
one of the most important in all Greece
to this day.

Towards the middle of the Fifteenth
century there were twenty-four
religious communities, but today
only four monasteries suspended
between heaven and earth are
still occupied: Hagios Stefanos,
which houses nuns, Hagia Trias,
Varlaam and Great Meteoron
which are inhabited by monks.

The monasteries of Mount Athos

The secret monasteries of Mount
Athos are still active today.
These sites are entirely devoted
to the Virgin Mary, the only female
presence tolerated there. Access
to Mount Athos is in fact strictly
forbidden to women and children
and is permitted only to men
(who must be over 21 years of age).
Those applying for permission
to visit the sites must demonstrate
a sincere religious interest

in the holy mountain, and authorisation
to enter Mount Athos is granted to only
ten outsiders a day who can thus enjoy
the privilege of being able to admire
the treasure of the monasteries.

Olympia, cradle of the sacred flame

The first Olympic games were organised by King Iphistos in 776 BC. At these games athletes could compete against one another at throwing the discus and the javelin, wrestling and running races; the chariot races were held at the hippodrome.

Since 1896, all the Olympic Games of the modern age

have marked their opening moment with the arrival in the host country of the bearer of the sacred flame, carried in relays all the way from where it was lit in ancient Olympia.

The southern Peloponnese

*Standing
on a rock
battered
by the waves
at the southernmost tip of the Peloponnese
peninsula, the citadel of Monemvassia
was once linked to the continent by no more
than a narrow strip of land. Hence
its name, which means "sole approach way"
in Greek. Its castles, ramparts and ancient
dwellings still seem to defy the passing
of time.
The statue of Leonidas, King of the city
of Sparta, is a tribute to this warrior's sacrifice
in defending the pass of Thermopylae against the vastly
superior numbers of the Persian army.*

The Byzantine city of Mistra

*Close to Sparta and to Mount Taygetos in Laconia, the city
of Mistra was the Byzantine capital of the Peloponnese
for two centuries. Even though it looks like a ghost-town
today, the city's ruined churches half-hidden among
the foliage and the fortress with its crumbling walls still
exert a powerful fascination over the visitor. The fortified
castle of Mistra was built in 1492 by the Franks
who sought to control the region.
The church of Hodegetria in the monastery
of Brontochion, at Mistra, was
founded in the Fourteenth century.
Its decorations were executed by
artists who came from Constantinople
(the ancient Byzantium),
and although these Fourteenth and
Fifteenth century Mistra paintings
have been damaged by the passing of
time — or the passing of Mistra's
conquerors — they still retain all their
wealth of expression nonetheless.*

Epidaurus, the magic of the theatre

◆◆◆◆◆◆◆◆◆◆◆◆◆◆◆◆◆◆◆

*The ancient theatre
of Epidaurus, built in the Fourth
century BC, was regarded
as its greatest wonder.
Two millennia later, it is still
one of the great
masterpieces
of the Greek
heritage. The theatre has now been restored,
and can seat up to 14,000 people. Its acoustics
are of such high quality that the slightest
murmur uttered on the stage can be heard
right up to the top of the terracing. Each
summer, from mid-June to the beginning
of September, delighted theatre-lovers come to the festival
of Epidaurus to enjoy lyric performances or see the plays
of Sophocles and Euripides.*

Along the islands of the Dodecanese

In the south-east Aegean Sea,
between Crete and Asia Minor, lie
the islands of the Dodecanese.
Although these islands have suffered
numerous periods of occupation
during the course of their history, they
have kept their spirit and their
attachment to Greece alive through
the years to the present day.
The beautiful island of Symi lying
to the south-east of Kos

is heavily frequented by tourists who come
from Rhodes for the day. Steps climb up
from the natural port of Egialos,
one of the most beautiful in Greece,
to the high town or Chora with
its picturesque maze of alleyways.
The people of this island are famous
for their boat-building talents, and legend
would have it that it was they who built the Argo for Jason
and his celebrated Argonauts.

Patmos, the island of the Apocalypse

To the north of the archipelago lies
the island of Patmos, site
of the cave where at the end
of the First century AD Saint John
is thought to have written
his prophetic Apocalypse, the last book
of the Gospel. The imposing monastery
of Agios Ioanis Theologos, founded
in his memory in the Eleventh century, dominates the whole
island; this veritable citadel of God is surrounded by
ramparts and encloses treasures of Byzantine art within
its walls. After Easter, the second most important holiday
celebrated in Greece is that of Panayia – the Assumption
of the Virgin Mary, on August 15. Some Greeks make

a pilgrimage
to Patmos
at this time
to pay homage
to Saint John
the Evangelist
and gather
together in the
famous cave of
the Apocalypse.

Crete – the other continent …

Poseidon, god of the sea, made
a gift of a magnificent white
bull to Minos, King of Crete. One
day Minos' wife Pasiphaë gave
birth to a monster, half-man
and half-bull: the Minotaur, fruit of her unnatural union
with the animal. This creature, which fed on human flesh,
was hidden away in a labyrinth designed
by the architect Daedalus. Minos demanded
that the city of Athens deliver fourteen young
people to him every three
years to feed to the monster.

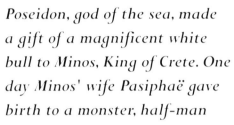

It was then that Theseus, son
of Aegeus the King of Athens,
decided to avenge his city's
honour by killing the Minotaur.
King Minos' daughter Ariadne fell
in love with Theseus and enabled him
to find his way out of the labyrinth
thanks to a thread she had unwound
through its maze of passageways.

Impressions

of

Greece

Printing Grafica Editoriale - Bologna
Dépôt légal : October 1998
(Printed in Italy)

Monday 22 May 2000

Outward Bound Journey

As ever we were rushing around trying to remember all those last minute jobs (we forgot to get the washing in !!) Posted our keys next door for Ant to feed our lovely cats. We'll miss them for 2 weeks.

N and I had an argument about where Juliet lived. I said it was the house with the old car parked outside. This wasn't enough information for N. He stopped car and I ran up drive to see if it was the correct one but didn't need to as all the luggage was alongside the motor. Juliet came down and said we could leave 2C's while we dropped the tank at Josie's. Carry was acting all shy but we just ignored him r left him.

I gave Josie her birthday pressies (a book for her nuts and some nice coasters) then we were all ready to go. (Oh, after Josie had finished cleaning the loo!) We waved to Juliets in the rain, glad to be leaving it all behind. The mini bus arrived just after 8am. We finally got to B'ham Int around 10am because

of the usual rush hour traffic on the M6.
check in was easy & trouble free.